ANYONE CAN BE
A (PERFECT)

WITCH

Thunder Bay Press
An imprint of Printers Row Publishing Group
THUNDER BAY 9717 Pacific Heights Blvd, San Diego, CA 92121
P·R·E·S·S www.thunderbaybooks.com • mail@thunderbaybooks.com

Correspondence regarding the content of this book should be sent to Thunder Bay
Press, Editorial Department, at the above address. Author and rights inquiries should
be addressed to

Vivida

The Vivida™ trademark is the property of White Star s.r.l.
www.vividabooks.com

Piazzale Luigi Cadorna, 6 - 20123 Milan, Italy
www.whitestar.it

Thunder Bay Press
Publisher: Peter Norton
Associate Publisher: Ana Parker
Editor: Dan Mansfield

ISBN: 978-1-6672-0148-1

Printed in Turkey

26 25 24 23 22   1 2 3 4 5

Publisher
Balthazar Pagani

Editing
Rachel Crawford

Graphic design, copy editing, layout
PEPE *nymi*

AMBROSIA HAWTHORN

ANYONE CAN BE
A (PERFECT)

WITCH

WITCHCRAFT FOR THE
MODERN WORLD

ILLUSTRATIONS BY

Giulia Varetto

THUNDER BAY
P·R·E·S·S
San Diego, California

CONTENTS

>>>>>>>>>>>>>> • <<<<<<<<<<<<<

INTRODUCTION

*D*o you hear it? The call of something deeper? Witchcraft, at its core, is an invitation.

It arises in the world around you, often showing itself in mysterious ways. It's akin to an outstretched hand, offering you a chance to manifest your desires, harness your inner power, and create positive change in your life. And the best part is that you already have the means you need to get started. You simply have to ask yourself if you will accept its offering. Will you rise and face yourself and the world around you?

Witchcraft isn't about being the best practitioner or elevating yourself above others. It's about being honest, genuine, and your true self. Witchcraft is growing, and it will continue to evolve because there is a demand for change.

Before I continue, I wanted to share a little about myself. My name is Ambrosia Hawthorn, and I am an experienced witch; author of *The Spell Book for New Witches*, *Seasons of Wicca*, and *The Wiccan Book of Shadows*; founder of *Witchology Magazine* (a magazine for modern witches); and witchcraft instructor at Venefica Cottage. I was born and raised in Northern California. I grew up believing in magic, and I'm here today because my curiosity and love of magic never left me.

Witchcraft isn't a secret society, nor is it reserved for any specific group. Anyone can be a witch. And yes, that means you. There's also no wrong way to be a witch. Your practice from day one is valid. You don't need to be initiated unless you're entering into a specific tradition or a coven, or if you want to perform your very own self-initiation ritual. These are all choices that you get to make for yourself. What's important is your dedication, and your respect for yourself, for others, and for your craft.

In this book, I'll explain how you can become a perfect witch in your own way. Positive change is possible; it's not outside your reach. Witchcraft is intuitive, guiding those who practice it to manifest their desires and goals. When paired with your intention, magic is a powerful force for creating change in your life.

By being here, reading this, you have felt its call—the pull of something more, inviting all seekers and curious minds alike.

You may have questions (as I did) about witchcraft, or you might simply be searching for new knowledge. In this book, I hope to offer in-depth answers and provide valuable information to equip you with the tools needed for a successful and rewarding path. Whether you're looking to practice more spells or to manifest change, you're in the right place.

I'm pleased that you'll be joining me as I introduce how to incorporate magic and witchcraft topics into your daily life, how to honor your inner power and cast spells. I wish you well on your witchcraft journey and hope the ideas, lessons, and philosophies in this book benefit you as they have me.

~ *Chapter 1* ~

AREAS OF LIFE

WHERE MAGIC COULD BE USEFUL

Y ou can find magic in the world around you, and in this section you'll learn how to incorporate more magic into your everyday life. Believe in yourself and set clear intentions to power your magic in your life.

Build confidence with witchcraft and manifest your desires in your life to create the changes you seek. You're well on your way to infusing witchcraft into the world around you and becoming a perfect witch.

You can experience magic in different areas of your life, such as your career, education, social life, fitness goals, and everyday activities.

These routine activities are exactly where magic is useful. These acts, when in tandem with your intent or magic mindfulness, are also called magical living. These sometimes-routine or monotonous tasks can be considered everyday rituals in which you can imbue magic for positivity and success.

A major goal of magic is to connect your inner and outer self and raise energy with a purpose. Your inner self consists of your intentions, emotions, feeling, and inner thoughts. Your outer self is your physical body and senses. At the end of this chapter, take special note how you might actively introduce magic in the different areas of your life.

Give the suggestions a try, and then see what works for you and what doesn't. The things that don't work are just as important as the things that do. You'll learn what's important to you and how to take what serves you, and disregard what doesn't.

This section has a lot of witchy goodness, from learning how to work with magical tools, palmistry, sigils, divination, breathwork, set a sacred space, and use magic daily. Magic can be cast at any time, but learning to work with cycles is a rewarding and powerful way to connect to magic in your life.

 # CAREER

Embrace the magic within yourself to solve problems at work, improve clarity and communication, and reduce stress. Career magic covers many areas, from promotion and job success to finding the right job. To craft a perfect career spell, mix any of the correspondences below, focus on your career desires, and add a pinch of confidence. You're well on your way to infusing witchcraft into your workplace and becoming a perfect witch.

HERBS AND SPICES: Brew a tea, sprinkle them into your lunch, or carry them in a pouch with other items. Try black pepper, rosemary, basil, cinnamon, bay leaves, or chamomile.

CRYSTALS: Place crystals in your workspace, carry them in your pocket or purse, wear them as jewelry, add them to a pouch, or hold them during meditation or visualization with your desires. Try citrine, sunstone, carnelian, sodalite, onyx, pyrite, amethyst, selenite, aventurine, tiger's eye, fluorite, jade, or ruby.

CANDLES AND COLORS: Dress with intent by donning specific colors, light a candle, or decorate your workspace to be a master of your craft. Try yellow for joy and group settings; orange for ambition, creativity, and courage; green for prosperity, ideas, and new ventures; brown for health, energy, and endurance.

MOON PHASES: Align your work-related projects or goals according to the moon phases. Use the new moon for beginnings and general career moves, or the waxing moon for goals and motivation.

EDUCATIONAL

Believe in yourself and set clear intentions to power your magic in your education. It's no secret that deadlines, exams, balancing priorities, and peer pressure can cause stress and strain in your life. Relieve those stressors and gain confidence in your power, regardless of what year or school you're in.

You don't have to have all the tools and ingredients to cast spells to be a witch. Below focuses on the magic already present at your fingertips. Work with what you have or is accessible and master your craft with minimal tools and objects.

PLANNER MAGIC: Try using a planner to schedule spells to the planetary energy so as to power your spells and manifest your desires. In your planner, datebook, or bullet journal, note the moon phases, planet retrogrades, sun-sign transitions, and the dates of planets from your own astrology chart.

PALMISTRY DIVINATION: Use your hands and explore palmistry divination and connecting to your intuition. All the lines and marks contain meaning or messages. To learn more about palmistry, search the Internet or your local bookstore to see what the different lines, fingers, and mounds mean. You'll get a glimpse at your heart, head, life, and fate.

SIGIL MAGIC: Draw sigils on blank pieces of paper for focus, success, and motivation. The easiest sigils to create are by producing shapes out of letters from affirmations like: "I am focused."

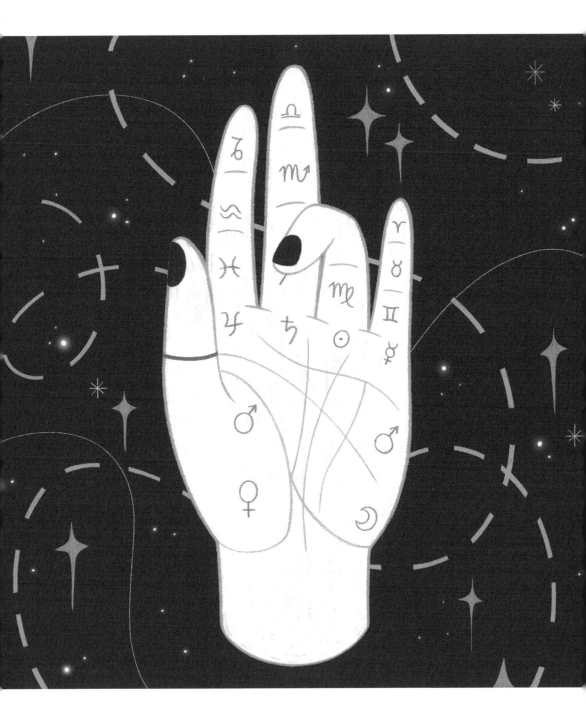

17

 # SOCIAL

Do you ever find yourself feeling nervous or uncomfortable because of an upcoming social situation? Perhaps you do before entering a room, going on a date or to an event, mingling with strangers, or starting conversations. Social settings, large or small, are a significant part of our lives; and whether you're an introvert or extrovert, witchcraft can help you get through those moments of nerves, uncertainty, or even fear.

CHARMS: Create a spell jar, sachet, or charm necklace with layered spices and herbs such as clove, black pepper, star anise, valerian root, licorice root, green tea, or ginger. These herbs all promote power and relaxation for managing social events.

AMULETS OR CRYSTALS: Use a necklace or crystal you have on hand by clearing old energies from the object through water or smoke, then pass your object through any of the above ingredients. Remember to set your intentions before wearing or carrying in social situations.

BREATHWORK: Use breathwork as a tool or ingredient-free way to regain composure and confidence in any social situation. Relax your shoulders and breathe in slowly through your nose for four seconds. Hold for two seconds and let your breath out for four seconds. Pair with an affirmation, or chant as you move between breathing phases such as "I am relaxed, I am strong, I am carefree."

FITNESS

Whether you play sports, go to the gym, or take a fitness class, witchcraft can help you achieve your goals. There are many ways to incorporate witchcraft into your fitness routine, and some of those ways are pre-fitness rituals and setting a sacred space. The main focus of witchy fitness is connecting your mind with your body and aiming to raise energy with a purpose. Workouts themselves consist of routines that aren't any different from a magical practice.

PRE-FITNESS RITUALS: Before any act, magical or mundane, it's important to prepare for your routines or rituals. Charge your workout water bottle by holding it and focus on your fitness intentions. Visualize the bottle being enveloped with your aura or white light. Practice relaxed,

deep breathing, and focus on your intention. With each sip, repeat your intention and feel the nourishing energy of the charged water blessing you with power and strength.

SACRED SPACE: Set an area that is sacred and safe wherever you will be practicing your fitness. This may be a gym, a sports field, or perhaps a small cubby in a fitness class. Set the start of your physical activity here. Take a sip of your charged water and feel its energy. Allow a moment to acknowledge your entrance into this space as a transition to your practice. This is often referred to as "setting the sacred space." Return to this space after your workout to release any excess energy through your feet, grounding yourself and "close or release the sacred space." A sacred space is safe and protects from external forces, thoughts, and unwanted energy.

≫ EVERYDAY ACTIVITIES ≪

Magic is useful in everyday activities like cooking, cleaning, sitting, commuting, or walking. These acts, when in tandem with your intent or magic mindfulness, are also called magical living. These sometimes-routine or monotonous tasks can be considered everyday rituals where you can imbue magic for positivity and success. Following routines of any kind allows you to work with cycles that are close to you. Harmonize your activities with the days of the week. Combining breathwork, meditation, visualization, or contemplation during these everyday acts can also help your mind stay rooted in the present and create awareness.

DAILY MAGIC: Embrace the magic of every day by working with cycles. Set your everyday tasks with the intentions of the magical times of the day below.

SUNRISE/MORNING: When the sun rises above the horizon. This time of the day is all about new beginnings, changes, health, employment, renewal, resurrection, and finding the right direction. It can also be very cleansing.

MIDMORNING: When the sun is growing in strength, bringing with it the magical power for growth, positive energy, resolutions, courage, harmony, happiness, strength, activity, projects, prosperity, and ideas.

MIDDAY: When the sun reaches its peak in the sky at noon. This is the best time of the day for magic related to health, physical energy, wisdom, and knowledge. It is also an excellent time to place your tools or crystals that need charging out in the sun.

AFTERNOON: The sun is heading back down, and the energy now is good for working on business matters, communication, clarity, travel, exploring, and anything professional.

SUNSET/EVENING: As the sun takes itself off down below the horizon, work magic for removing depression, stress, and confusion, letting go, releasing, or finding out the truth of a situation.

MIDNIGHT: Midnight is the start of a new twenty-four-hour day and is the time when spirit communication is at its strongest. Use this time for enhancing spirit work, psychic abilities, and stillness.

CENTERING
AND GROUNDING

Centering is when you reinforce your connection to yourself, which allows you to focus on the relationship to your energy, which will help you work with it. Centering often goes hand in hand with grounding, as these two techniques help you stay balanced and at energy equilibrium.

Center and ground yourself when you feel restless, overwhelmed, unfocused, forgetful, or your self-esteem is low. The easiest way to center and ground is through meditation and visualization.

CENTERING: Find a quiet place to sit and begin with long, slow, and deep breaths, in and out. Once you're relaxed, visualize your energy. Gently rub your hands together and slowly pull them apart, focusing on the space between them. Any tingling sensations you feel are threads of energy waiting to be used.

GROUNDING: Sit in a comfortable position and begin focusing on your breath. Next, visualize all the excess energy you've built leaving your body, dispersing into the earth.

PALMISTRY LINES

*T*here are four major lines you can read on your palm. These are your heart, head, life, and fate lines. The lines on your palm can either be defined and easy to read or broken, faded, or even missing altogether.

HEART

The heart line runs horizontally across the upper part of your palm. It gives us insight into your relationships, emotions, and potential for personal growth. The deeper the heart line, the deeper your love and affection.

HEAD

Next after the heart line is the head line, representing intellect and reasoning. A straight line reveals a more logical approach, where curves hint at creativity.

LIFE

The life line begins between your thumb and index finger and runs down toward the wrist. This line reveals your enthusiasm for life, not how long you will live.

FATE

The fate line is often a straight line that splits the palm into two sections. It deals with purpose and direction in life. A straight line is associated with a straightforward path.

~ *Chapter 2* ~

MAGIC WITH

PEOPLE

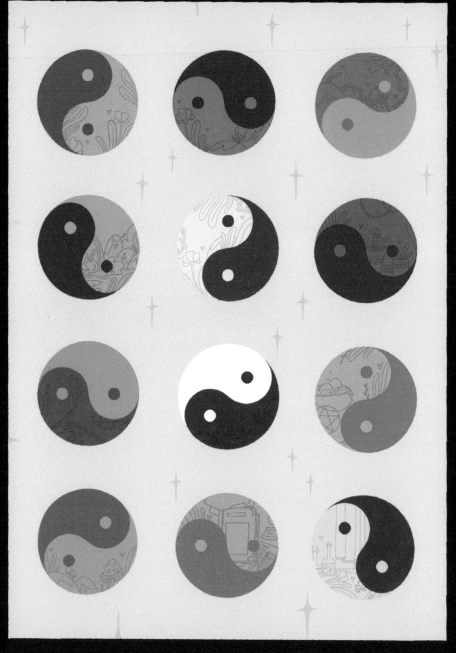

I n the previous section you learned how magic could help you with social situations or events, but that's just the beginning. Witchcraft can be helpful in many areas of your life, and this is especially true with relationships of all kinds. Whether it is regarding friends, family, partners, community, neighbors, or even enemies, when practicing any sort of magic it's essential to be mindful of how you create change or manipulate the energies around you.

Setting your boundaries and asking yourself clarifying questions are essential before you perform spells relating to others. Where do your ethics lie when it comes to casting spells involving others?

Casting spells for love is one of the most popular forms of magic used in witchcraft. But the ethics can be unclear. In your practice, do you feel they are ethical?

Identifying your spell ethics is essential to help you establish rules, principles, and values that you can base your craft on. It's important to find your sense of ethical direction in your daily life.

Philosopher Aristotle held discussions about ethics and reciprocity, which topic is now referred to as "The Ethic of Reciprocity." Its meaning is that anything you wish upon others should also be wished upon yourself. This is a social foundation for healthy relationships.

Wicca, a popular religion often associated with witchcraft, has its own cosmic law or law of return. This concept teaches that your deeds are revisited upon you threefold. Many practitioners adopt this concept to their own moral compass, and it's often recommended to new practitioners.

Before trying to control or manipulate others' emotions or paths, ask yourself if you'd be okay with another trying to manipulate or control you.

This section focuses on attracting, increasing, finding, healing, or accepting the connections in your life.

⋙ FRIENDS AND FAMILY ⋘

The desire to help loved ones is powerful. Mastering your magical practice can allow you to help your loved one overcome any situation. The most straightforward ways you can assist your friends and family are through charms, charged gifts, or candle spells.

CHARM BAGS OR JARS: Set the purpose of a charm and locate associated correspondences to use in a bag or jar. Does your loved one have insomnia? Combine lavender and mugwort in a muslin bag to create a sleep-charm bag-pillow for them. Perhaps a friend is stressed over his work. Combine food-grade herbs like chamomile, valerian, lemon balm,

and lavender in a jar, and gift with instructions to brew a stress-relieving tea that you've crafted and charged with your intentions.

CANDLES: When your family member or friend is in trouble, clear your mind, set your intentions, and light a candle for a specific purpose.

- **White:** Healing, peace, and truth

- **Purple:** Spiritual awareness, wisdom, and tranquility

- **Lavender:** Intuition, peace, and healing

- **Blue:** Meditation, healing, forgiveness, inspiration, fidelity, happiness, and communication

- **Green:** Money, fertility, luck, abundance, health, and success

- **Pink:** Positive self-love, friendship, harmony, and joy

- **Yellow:** Manifesting thoughts, confidence, goals, creativity, intelligence, and mental clarity

- **Orange:** Joy, energy, education, strength, and attraction

- **Red:** Passion, energy, love, lust, relationships, vitality, and courage

- **Black:** Protection, absorption, and banishing negative energy

 # PARTNERS

Whether you want to attract new love or strengthen your current bonds, performing magic related to attraction with tools and ingredients associated with love is beneficial. Love potions or philters are brews created with power and intention and have been used for centuries.

ATTRACTING NEW LOVE: Brew a love oil that you can wear to enhance attraction energies. To formulate a love oil, you can dilute a few drops of essential oils like rose, lemon, orange, bergamot, or ylang-ylang in carrier oils like jojoba, olive, or coconut oils before applying to your skin. Alternatively, you can use real dried herbs in a jar, but this process takes six to eight weeks to grow in strength.

STRENGTHENING CURRENT RELATIONSHIPS: Steep love-supporting herbs in an herbal tea or tisane that can be drunk to promote loving energies between you and a partner. Add up to three teaspoons of dried rose, hibiscus, and lavender in a tea ball or bag. Pour boiling water and let sit for about ten minutes. Decant and enjoy. If you desire to share with your loved one, offer the potion as a gift imbued with your own loving feelings. A gift given with sincerity is powerful in any circumstance.

COMMUNITY

At its origin, witchcraft has been practiced in a community setting, whether in a coven, circle, ritual group, or, recently, in online communities. The word *coven* comes from the Latin *convenire*, which means coming together. A coven's purpose is exactly that, to come together with like-minded individuals to work together on common intentions. These might be spells, rituals, celebrations, or sharing ideas. Today, many witches come together over the Internet and on social media and celebrate inclusion and revere the world.

INCLUSION: In its past, witchcraft has been seen as a refuge for empowering and inclusivity and the non-mainstream. Like a sacred space, witches often create physical or online spaces where others can feel safe and accepted. To practice magic in your own community, seek other communities of witches or create your own. Share your beliefs, craft, and ideas with others who are interested in listening.

NATURAL WORLD: Witches live in tandem with nature, celebrating the Earth's natural cycles through the seasons, planetary cycles, and the waxing and waning energies of the year. Between the summer and winter solstices in the Northern Hemisphere, solar energy is waning. Practice magic relating to rest, relaxation, slumber, remembrance, gratitude, letting go, and banishing. Between the winter and summer solstices, solar energy is waxing, or growing. Practice magic relating to rebirth, renewal, growth, vitality, action, and new beginnings.

NEIGHBORS

While we can choose our friends, we often cannot choose our neighbors. Almost everyone has or has had neighbors in their life. These connections are more important than just being able to borrow a cup of sugar when you're in a pinch. And while you may or may not have a relationship with your neighbors, these connections are key to your security and peace of mind. Practice being a perfect witch through acceptance, inclusion, and respect.

KITCHEN MAGIC: Cook with intention and use ingredients to promote intended properties like peace, welcoming, acceptance, and respect. The easiest way to practice kitchen magic is to use spices with intention. Take a look at what you might already have in your kitchen pantry. Each spice has its own energy and correspondences. Make a list of the herbs and spices you have and research their magical properties. Make a list and plan some meals. When you've created something with intention, invite your neighbor for a meal.

Not sure you're ready to cook something for a neighbor? You could instead invite them for tea and coffee. Tea is associated with cleansing, clarifying, new beginnings, and reflection, while coffee is associated with grounding, getting past blockages, and peace of mind.

⫸ ENEMIES OR RIVALS ⫷

Not everyone has an enemy or a rival, but perhaps there's someone who you feel challenges, competes, opposes, or confronts you in any area of your life. While competitions aren't a bad thing, they can quickly become toxic or unhealthy. These situations can often lead to pressure or unnecessary stress in your life. Witchcraft can be very beneficial to assist with handling rivals without causing harm. When thinking of rivals and witchcraft, it's easy to think about hexes, curses, or anything considered harmful, dark, or evil. What most don't realize is that witchcraft can be used for understanding, trust, bonds, and healing just as effectively. Throughout time, witchcraft has been given the reputation of being evil or being used unjustly. We can break down these barriers by learning how to use magic and witchcraft ethically for good.

COMPETITIONS OR RIVALRY: Create an incantation or chant that you can easily repeat throughout times of competition or contests. Focus on empowering yourself or creating positivity. Try resting your hand over your heart and chant: "I invoke peace, courage, and confidence and release envy, hate, and jealousy."

BULLYING: Craft a poppet or spell doll to take your place as the victim of bullying. Poppets are a form of sympathetic magic that will direct the focus off you and onto your intended object. Cut out a doll shape from one of your old T-shirts. Sew along the edges and, just before closing, turn inside out. You can be as creative as you'd like with your doll. The important part of poppet creation is using things that belong to you and are infused with your energy. Fill the doll with rosemary for protection and warding and red pepper for power and protection.

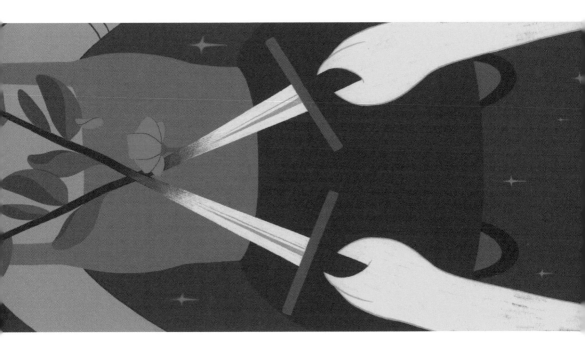

THE ORIGIN
OF SPELLCASTING

The term "spell" originates from the Anglo-Saxon word *spel*, which means "saying" or "story." Casting spells has been prevalent throughout history. The cultures of ancient Greece and Rome used spells to curse, protect, heal, bind, and invoke. These cultures crafted curse tablets, offerings to deities, protection amulets, and herbal potions. Many wore necklaces and objects engraved with letters and symbols to protect themselves from evil and sickness. In simple terms, spells have been used throughout time to fulfill wishes and desires.

Another component of spellcasting throughout time is the use of object correspondences. You can think of a correspondence as a timeless link to ancient myths and deities, history, and folklore. Using spell correspondences helps you take a glimpse back in time and connect to the deeper meanings found in the objects around you. These spell correspondences refer to the original connection between an object's symbolism and purpose.

A WITCH'S PANTRY

*B*eyond the magical tools that witches use, there's also the witch's pantry, which consists of herbs, spices, botanicals, and oils. Many of these items can be found in your local grocery store, and less-common ingredients can be found in witchcraft specialty supply stores or ordered online. Don't let the idea of an entire pantry intimidate you. You probably have some of the ingredients in your kitchen already. Below are common herbs that you might have in your kitchen cupboard.

- **BASIL:** Luck, prosperity, harmony, money, peace, purification
- **BLACK PEPPER:** Protection, banishing negativity and jealousy, warding
- **CINNAMON:** Spirituality, love, protection, money, power, success, strength
- **CUMIN:** Protection, love, fidelity, exorcism, abundance, anti-theft
- **GINGER:** Balance, grounding, love, clarity, money, success, power, stability
- **OREGANO:** Protection, creativity, travel, freedom, love, happiness, dreams
- **ROSEMARY:** Cleansing, strength, protection, memory, healing, money
- **THYME:** Healing, purification, courage, sleep, love, psychic abilities, dreams

~ Chapter 3 ~

MAGIC IN EVERYDAY
LIFE

E mbrace the perfect witch within you, starting with your home. In Chapter 1, we covered where in our lives magic is useful. Looking at our daily routines is an excellent way to practice incorporating magic. Beyond school, the gym, your job, social settings, or daily activities, magic helps us infuse intentions into every aspect of our lives. In this section, we'll go even deeper into the areas of your life where magic exists and can be connected to.

Your home is where you can relax, recharge, and be yourself. Practicing magic in your home allows you to incorporate manifestation magic, clearing and cleansing, protection, comfort, harmony, and balance in your life. Master your craft in your home to inspire your own creativity, create safe spaces, whip something up in your kitchen, tend to your garden, or harness the tools you already have within your reach. And the best part? You'll discover along the way that the perfect witch is already there, waiting to be tapped into.

House magic, or magic in the home, is a great way to use minimal ingredients or tools already available to you, and you'll be surprised at how confident you'll feel. Learn to create with intention, set boundaries, and weave magic into the core of your home. Look more closely at the magical properties of the items around you to face the world, becoming more confident and empowered.

⟫ CRAFT AND CREATIVITY ⟪

Do you ever wish for more creativity? Set an area dedicated to your hobbies, arts, or crafts and combine it with your intention setting. Setting the space allows for an opportunity for creative discipline and thinking. Whether you have a studio or just two feet of space in your living room, making a space for creativity to thrive is essential for manifestation magic of any kind. Do you ever feel like you suffer from artist's or writer's block? Allow yourself time and space for attracting positivity and creative growth.

FIRE MAGIC: Connect with the element of fire and its properties of inspiration and action by lighting a candle or incense. Try either a yellow or an orange candle for creativity, or use cinnamon in your incense.

BOOK OF SHADOWS: Start recording all the spells, recipes, rituals, and/or any relevant witchcraft practices you've enjoyed in a Book of Shadows (BOS). A Book of Shadows is a sacred tool that witches personalize and use to document anything that relates to their practice. Think of this as a creative way to document your journey as a witch.

SACRED SPACES

Learn to set sacred or creative spaces to practice your magic free from negative energy. Most witchcraft today is practiced in a sacred space or an area of the home. While you can cast spells and rituals elsewhere, the home is where most of us feel the most safe and secure. You can set a sacred space in any room of the home; so whether you live in a one-bedroom apartment or a four-bedroom house, you're the one who decides where you want your sacred space to be. That means if you want to create a space in a closet or dedicate an entire table, the choice is yours. You can cast all kinds of spells and rituals in the home, but it's essential to cleanse before each magical working or whenever you feel called to do so.

CLEANSING MAGIC: Just like physical clutter, the home accumulates a lot of stagnant and unwanted energies, so routinely clearing them away will help you feel more refreshed. Practice cleansing your home often, especially after a sickness, an argument, a new transition, or if you simply feel off in some way. Use an incense blend or bundle to cleanse, or craft a cleansing spray by mixing salt, witch hazel, and essential oils with water in a spray bottle. Use essential oils like clary sage or palo santo for extra cleansing power.

 # KITCHEN

Whether you're headed to the kitchen to make a cup of tea, cook a meal, or clean, magic is abundant in all areas of the kitchen. Similar to a sacred space, the kitchen is also a unique sanctuary for a witch. If you have ingredients, the possibilities that you can create are endless. Most kitchen witches spend time accumulating spices, spell oils, or other do-it-yourself projects for healing and cleansing.

BLESSINGS: Bless each item you make, and infuse your intentions. Before cooking a meal, clear away old energies with cleansing magic mentioned in sacred spaces, and begin selecting your ingredients with intention. Try looking up the correspondences for each item and be mindful of what they represent.

- **Apples:** Love, prosperity
- **Apricots:** Love, relaxation
- **Avocados:** Fertility, beauty, love
- **Bananas:** Fertility, potency, prosperity
- **Beans:** Protection, reconciliations
- **Berries:** Healing, love, protection, strength
- **Carrots:** Fertility, love, passion
- **Celery:** Mental and psychic powers, concentration
- **Citrus:** Health, happiness, love
- **Coconuts:** Protection, purification
- **Corn:** Luck, prosperity, divination, protection
- **Cucumbers:** Healing, fertility, beauty
- **Lettuce:** Protection, healing, divination
- **Onions:** Prosperity, stability, protection, banishing
- **Peas:** Love, wealth
- **Pomegranates:** Divination, luck, wealth, wishes, fertility
- **Potatoes:** Protection, poppet magic, healing, strength, grounding
- **Rice:** Blessing, money, prosperity, fertility, protection, wealth
- **Tomatoes:** Love, health, prosperity, passion, protection
- **Zucchini:** Prosperity, protection

INDOOR OR OUTDOOR GARDEN

Do you have one plant, or twenty? Or perhaps you have a garden with herbs, or maybe you often purchase flowers from a local market? Having and tending to plants of any kind allows you to connect with the natural world and its energy. A garden is a great resource to have, but that doesn't mean you have to have growing plants that you can forage. You might have an indoor herb garden, or you might simply enjoy the occasional ornamental flowers. Getting your hands on real plants is a wonderful way to use them in your practice.

HOUSE PLANTS: Nurture your plant with your intentions and create mini rituals for growth, manifestation, or other goals important to you. Propagate a cactus, purchase a plant, or grow one from a seed at the beginning of any new transition in your life and infuse your intentions. You could also turn your watering into a mini ritual and pair it with a chant or affirmation like "No matter what comes my way, I can handle it and succeed."

DRIED BOTANICALS: Hang flowers or bouquets upside down to dry and preserve their shape. These dried botanicals can then be used in charm bags, spell oils, bath salts, candle dressings, or incense bundles that pair with your intentions.

 # BATHROOM

The bathroom is the perfect place to practice self-love and beauty magic, or to begin trying glamour magic. In the bathroom, you have access to the element of water, tools that you use daily, and mirrors. Allow your bathroom to become a safe space that you can connect to with your body and boost your confidence to manifest your desires or intentions.

GLAMOUR MAGIC: Harness the clothes and products you have, to boost your confidence and combine with your intentions to enhance your inner power. Try using tools like makeup, perfume, oils, crystals, or jewelry to charge and imbue with energy.

BATH MAGIC: Add a cup of Epsom salts to your next bath and set the energy by lighting a candle or adding a few drops of a relaxing essential oil like lavender. You can also incorporate meditation, visualization, or affirmation chants to match your intention.

MIRROR SPELLS: Mirrors are excellent for absorbing, powering, or deflecting magic. Mirrors can often harbor negative connotations, but they aren't dangerous. When working with mirrors, come from a place of positivity and strength of mind. After your next shower, use your finger to create and draw a sigil on the mirror for confidence or self-love. You can also focus on your image in the mirror and repeat an affirmation like "I am powerful, I am confident, I love myself."

CLEANSING BASICS

*A*ll magical tools need to be cleansed before you can use them. If you don't cleanse the residual energy from objects, you might unintentionally draw upon someone else's energy.

- **WATER:** Water is and always has been an excellent cleansing element. You can use any water and even opt for charged waters such as moon or floral for an added power boost.
- **SALT:** Salt cleanses and charges objects, but be careful that the item won't rust.
- **SOAP:** Natural soap is a great way to remove grime or hard-to-banish energy clinging to an object. Begin with castile soap, as it's not too harsh.

- **FIRE:** Fire-cleansing works great for metal objects. Light a candle and pass the item quickly over the flame, being careful not to let it get too hot.
- **SMOKE:** Burning incense or herbs is an excellent way to cleanse objects. All manner of dried plants, resins, and herbal powders can be used, including rosemary, lavender, sage, thyme, bay, catnip, mint, pine, and more.

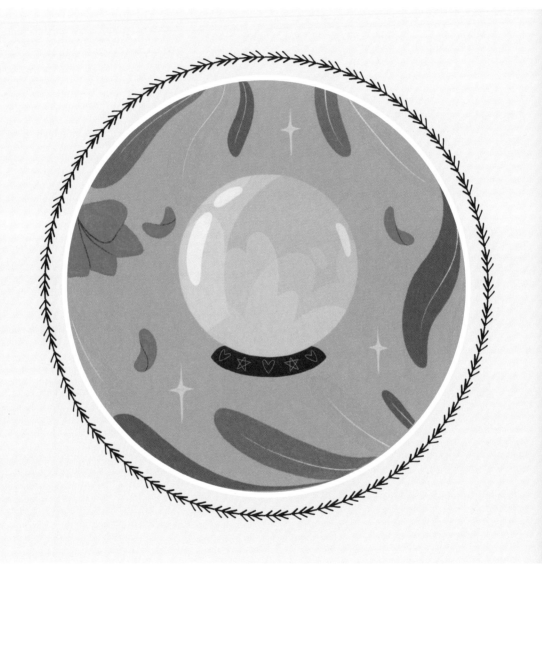

~ Chapter 4 ~

DIVINATION AND

INTUITION

Divination is the process of seeking knowledge about the unknown. It's a witch's way to gain insight and answers to life's questions. Divining is a powerful tool with many options to fit your practice. If one method doesn't work for you, don't give up: you can try another.

Most witches start with tarot, but there are also oracle decks, casting stones, runes, ogham staves, scrying, dowsing, numerology, astrology, intuition, messages, and automatic writing. In the section below, we'll dive into these different divination areas, and you'll get to see which one sounds right to you.

One of the biggest misconceptions is that you have to be psychic to practice divination, but this isn't true. Anyone willing to start trusting their intuition can practice the many forms of divination. While you may not be a psychic from birth, you can still master divination practices.

Intuition is your gut instinct, or the innate voice of your consciousness. This feeling gives us the ability to know something without a logical reason. Have you ever had a "bad feeling" about something but didn't know why? Or maybe when you last got dressed to go out, you had the feeling you should wear one outfit over all the others? These are all instances of your intuition instinctively sending you a message.

All you have to do is be present and start listening. You'll be pleasantly surprised by how much your intuition has to say. Your intuition is present to keep you safe and happy, warning you of threats or negative energy while also knowing what's in your heart when it might not be so clear.

Your intuition wants you to see past logical reasoning and worry, and do what feels right. Allow your intuition to guide you and feel a deeper connection and awareness to yourself.

TAROT AND ORACLE DECKS

Tarot and oracle decks are card-based divination systems. The main difference between these two types of decks is their structure. Tarot decks are almost always seventy-eight cards and are made up of the twenty-two Major Arcana cards and fifty-six Minor Arcana cards. The Minor Arcana are further divided into four suits: cups, wands, swords, and pentacles. On the other hand, oracle often doesn't have rigid structures, and you might have anywhere from twenty cards to a hundred. Neither deck type is better than the other, and many witches often read both systems.

CARD OF THE DAY: To start learning any deck of your choice, start by pulling one card of the day and journal its message. To know its message, give yourself a few minutes to stare at the card. Note the colors, symbols, what's going on in the card, and how it makes you feel. Your intuition will help you get to the card's meaning and what it could mean for your day.

You can also read the little booklet that comes with the deck, but the booklet is purely logical, not your intuition. When you're ready, start pulling more cards to combine into a larger reading. Some common spreads include between three and twelve cards, but you can have any number for a reading. The more cards you add, the more meanings you'll have to combine.

CASTING STONES, RUNES, AND OGHAM STAVES

Casting stones, also called lithomancy, is the divination practice of reading stones. They are the easiest stone divination method to learn, as you don't need to learn a unique alphabet like the runes or ogham. The stones used in casting are smooth stones or tumbled crystals.

Casting stones can be inscribed with any symbol that has meaning to you, and you can use any number of stones. The key is to assign importance to your own set.

Runes, on the other hand, are the Elder Futhark alphabet, consisting of twenty-four letters. These letters are then inscribed on smooth stones. Their meanings are read much like card-based systems.

The ogham is an Early Medieval alphabet and consists of twenty letters. These are often inscribed into pieces of wood and used in the same way as casting stones or runes. This form of divination is known as xylomancy.

What all three of these divination types have in common is the reading method. You can put the stones or staves in a bag, shake them, then pour them on a table. Look to see which symbols are face up to read.

CRAFT YOUR OWN: Create your own set of casting stones. Collect a set number of stones or tumbled crystals, and use a permanent marker to draw symbols important to you or your practice.

SCRYING AND DOWSING

Tap into your latent psychic abilities through other divination practices like scrying and dowsing. Scrying is the art of gazing into reflective surfaces, water, or fire to receive intuitive messages or visions. The art of gazing into a crystal ball to see the future is a popular example of scrying divination. Visions or messages received during a scrying session often relate to future events.

MIRROR OR CRYSTAL SCRYING: Also referred to as catoptromancy, this is a form of gazing into polished obsidian, quartz, or a mirror to see words or visions appear in your mind's eye.

WATER SCRYING: Also called hydromancy, this method of scrying allows you to gaze into a bowl of water for messages. You can also tap the surface of the water with a magical tool like a wand to create ripples. These ripples can also bring intuitive messages.

FIRE SCRYING: Also called pyromancy, this is when you gaze into a candle and watch the fire flick and dance to see what messages or shapes appear to you.

DOWSING: This is a form of divination that uses an object to receive and transmit energy. The common form of dowsing we see today is with a pendulum and board. A pendulum board often has the alphabet and words like "yes," "no," and "maybe." A pendulum is a weighted piece of crystal or metal suspended from a pivot to swing freely.

NUMEROLOGY AND ASTROLOGY

While numerology and astrology are two different topics, they both study meanings and how they relate to our everyday lives. Astrology studies celestial motion and changes, and astrologers use birth or event charts to get insights into the past and present. Numerology studies numbers and their meaning, and numerologists study the numbers dominant in one's life.

Both practices use birth data of a recipient. Witches use these divination practices because they have spiritual and magical significance. As a witch, you can use numerology and astrology in your spell work.

ASTROLOGY: Write down your place of birth and birth date and time and find a free chart tool or app online to pull your own astrology chart to begin reading astrology. Look for your sun, moon, and rising sign to learn about your personality. Your sun sign is your identity, your moon sign is emotions and needs, and your rising is your personality and impression on others. You may want to customize spells to your planets' placements in your chart.

NUMEROLOGY: Take your date of birth and log it into a life-path calculator online to get your number to reveal traits about your personality, outlook, and challenges in life. Once you have your life-path number, try incorporating that number into a spell's chants or ingredients.

OTHER DIVINATION FORMS

There are countless methods of divination systems for receiving messages. Most message systems end in "-ancy," which is Latin for "quality of state" and describes ways to use objects or events through which to gain insight or messages. The suffix "-ancy" is a great identifier for different types of divination. Many witches actively grow their psychic or intuitive abilities like a muscle. It's also important to note that divination doesn't come easily to all, and each method requires patience and practice to develop.

Check this list to see if any of these forms call out to you to try. Divination helps power your intuition for spell work.

- **Aeromancy:** Clouds, birds, sky, weather patterns
- **Aleuromancy:** Flour or baked goods
- **Astragalomancy:** Bones or dice with symbols
- **Axinomancy:** Axe marks in wood
- **Belomancy:** Drawing arrows marked with messages
- **Bibliomancy:** Opening a book to a random page
- **Cartomancy:** Using playing cards
- **Ceromancy:** Melted-wax messages
- **Chiromancy:** Palmistry or hand divination
- **Cleromancy:** Luck or casting lots
- **Dactyliomancy:** Using rings
- **Geomancy:** Geometric lines or shapes
- **Gyromancy:** Walking in circles or spinning
- **Hydromancy:** Water or liquid
- **Lecanomancy:** Form of hydromancy, using a bowl of water
- **Lithomancy:** Runes or casting stones
- **Necromancy:** Spirit communication
- **Oneiromancy:** Dream messages
- **Onomancy:** Letters of a name
- **Oomancy:** Using eggs
- **Ornithomancy:** Flight of birds
- **Osteomancy:** Bones
- **Phyllomancy:** Leaf divination
- **Psephomancy:** Pebble divination
- **Pyromancy:** Flames or fire
- **Rhabdomancy:** Dowsing rods
- **Tasseomancy:** Tea-leaf reading
- **Xylomancy:** Wood divination

YOUR INNER POWER

*W*hen terms like raising power, building power, or even harnessing your inner power come about, they refer to the energy that is already within you and how much power you possess. Power is the practical art of channeling energy for your use. When you begin manipulating and channeling energy from the world around you, you are, in a sense, building up your own personal power. Through this manipulation, you can influence or control the energy around you to cast stronger spells.

Spells work off your personal or inner power and the magical tools or specific events you use. Spells are what also allow you to practice magic. They help you create change in your life and bring out more confidence in yourself.

For example, have you ever noticed why some spells recommend that you cast on a specific day? Or time of the year? This is because of the energy associated with that specific day or event.

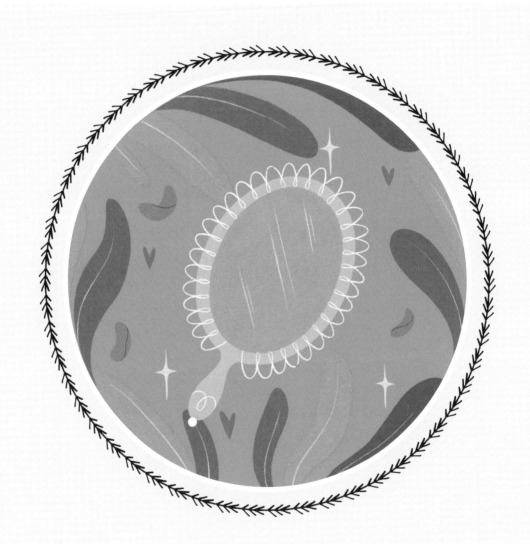

~ Chapter 5 ~

MAGIC WITH
THE SELF

The "self" is a term that can be broken down into different concepts or constructs involving identity, image, esteem, confidence, and efficacy—asking questions about your perception of yourself and your beliefs. By recognizing these concepts or constructs, you can identify who you are as a person and witch.

Witchcraft, at its core, is about healing, acceptance, and transformation of your mind, emotions, physical body, and spiritual self. Spells involving self-love and self-care are the perfect examples of practicing magic with the self. Practicing magic with the self is the ideal way to master your craft and build an empowering practice.

The early witches in history were wise women or natural healers who created change and nurtured and cared for others. These figures were often at the forefront of persecution generated out of the misunderstandings and fear of the unknown. Today, we are often faced with the notion that witches are evil and dark.

Healing is a process of becoming and restoring. Whether you're looking to begin your journey into witchcraft or advance your craft in the magic of the self, this chapter will help you take action and grow as a witch. Allow your magic to shine brilliantly, free from restrictions or fear.

In this section, we'll dive into the different ways you can intertwine who you are as a witch and who you believe you are. Healing, like witchcraft, is a lifelong journey of learning, discovery, and acceptance of your inner and outer natures.

SELF-IMAGE, HEALING, AND RELEASE

How do you see yourself, and what do you imagine that others see in you? What you see and imagine directly influences other aspects of yourself. You can take a stand and decide right now to release negative self-image and empower the positive for healing. Once you begin to release and heal, you not only feel better about yourself but also become more resilient.

MIRROR MAGIC: Use a mirror to cast an Affirm Your Worth Spell. To do this, use a plain compact handheld mirror and draw a pentacle or custom sigil on the back of it. Then open it to look at your reflection and begin listing qualities you know you have. Repeat often. Each time you state your list, add one more positive quality.

CLEANSING MAGIC: Cleansing away negative thoughts and feelings is a great way to banish unwanted thoughts or energy from yourself and your space. Formulate your own loose incense blend or dried herb bundle, or use an incense-stick scent intuitively. When choosing your scents, look for more blends that list their ingredients, and avoid synthetic materials. Allow yourself to be present and visualize the smoke pushing out wisps of negativity.

SELF-ESTEEM, MIND, AND OBSTACLES

When working with the mind, you may face obstacles, doubts, and endless opinions from yourself or others. Value has a big part in this, as it plays on your self-image and your assessment of yourself. Do you celebrate your attributes, characteristics, and abilities? Or do you struggle with seeing yourself with only a few good qualities, characteristics, or skills? Let witchcraft aid you in celebrating yourself daily, and be present in the moment. You have your own special qualities, characteristics, and skills that set you apart from anyone else. Your magical practice helps pave a path that's uniquely yours.

CRYSTAL GRID: Select crystals to create a grid that you charge and activate for specific intentions. Create a grid using your intuition with the number of stones you have, then hover your hand above each one, call its property, state your intention, and focus on your desire. Visualize your energy and see it charging and activating each stone. Work with the crystals you have, or try any of the crystals below. Use stones that are pink, red, orange, yellow, brown, or clear to give your mind and self-esteem a boost of empowering energy.

SELF-ESTEEM: Agate, calcite, carnelian, citrine, jasper, clear or rose quartz, rhodonite, tiger's eye, and sunstone are great options.

SELF-IDENTITY, EMOTIONS, AND ACCEPTANCE

Your self-identity is closely tied to what represents you as an individual. It combines your interests, abilities, experiences, traits, memories, and hobbies. Spend time with yourself and your craft to nurture your connection to your practice. You'll find that your emotions will become more balanced, and acceptance of yourself will have the opportunity to flourish.

WITCHY CRAFTS: Become skilled with what you enjoy making. Try making poppets, charm bags, magical teas, incense bundles, or other tangible items. Are you a secret resin artist? Savvy knitter or tea enthusiast? Become skilled in that area of your craft. This practice will allow you to become more acquainted with the perfect witch within you. Not sure what direction to go in? Spend time discovering what you enjoy. Brainstorm and make a list of what excites you.

COMMUNITY: Join groups, circles, or online communities related to your interests. Try looking through social media or online search engines for other witches or individuals that have your interests. Take the initiative to partake in activities that interest you.

SELF-CONFIDENCE AND THE PHYSICAL BODY

While the previous areas where witchcraft can be beneficial focus a lot on the mind, harnessing the witch within you can also be physical. Your sense of touch comes from pressure, temperature, vibration, or pain. These sensations connect you to the natural world and ground you. To get started working with the physical magic around you and building your self-confidence, try coming in contact with the elements below.

GROUNDING: Release excess energy from your spell work or interactions with others by taking your shoes off the next time you're standing

on grass, soil, or sand. Digging your toes into the earth while you close your eyes and focus on the sensations will connect you physically to the element of earth. Feel the support of the earth and its nudge toward confidence.

BATH MAGIC: Take a bath or shower to directly feel water's presence and connect with its cleansing, healing, and refreshing properties. Take a moment to feel the recharging and uplifting effects of the water element. Allow yourself to feel confident and refreshed.

WIND AND WARMTH: The two elements not easily touched can still be felt. Sit in front of a fire and feel its warmth envelop you, warming and encouraging you. Stand still on a windy day and connect to the air's wisdom and changing energy.

SELF-EFFICACY, SPIRIT, AND BELIEF

Beyond the physical or material, we have the spiritual. This is how you can connect to your path, thoughts, or beliefs. Witchcraft works in harmony with self-efficacy to celebrate your belief in yourself and your power. Witchcraft can manifest change in your life; and, when paired with spiritual practices, you receive guidance, allow yourself to be present, live intentionally, and become open to positivity or gratitude.

JOURNALING: Take time out of your busy schedule to write down any thoughts, feelings, struggles, questions, experiences, or reflections you may have. If you journal before you start your day, write down your intentions. If you journal at the end of your day, write what you achieved.

PRAYER: Whether to a higher being or your inner power, taking time to ask for help or guidance is a personal way to practice connecting to the magic within you. Pair your prayer with a ritual such as a new moon for deeper clarity and guidance about your direction.

MEDITATION: Seeking guidance through prayer is asking, while meditation focuses solely on listening. Meditate regularly to listen to your mind and body. Combine meditation with an event like the full moon for focus and manifest.

SPELL LIMITATIONS AND EXPIRATION

Before you begin casting spells, take time to understand that spells aren't "get out of jail free" cards. Spells have limitations and can expire. They cannot instantly fix all the problems you may want them to: they take energy, time, effort, focus, and belief to work.

They are also temporary manipulations of energy, not permanent ones. While there are no specific expiration dates assigned to your spells, they slowly begin to fade as soon as they are cast. Most spells can last either a few days, weeks, or months.

Spells can fade more quickly or more slowly depending on the amount of energy you use. You can think of the energy used in spells like a battery. This also means that if you continuously supply energy into a spell through recharging or repeating it, you can keep the spell from fading.

Spells can be as powerful as you are, and their limitations rely on you, your intentions, and your power.

PERSONALIZING YOUR PRACTICE

*P*ersonalize your practice by connecting with your senses. You can use these senses to customize your altar table or sacred space.

SIGHT: You can add things like crystals, statues, pictures, color-themed items, candles, or anything else that helps you get yourself transitioned into a new state of mind.

SMELL: You can do things like burning incense, diffusing essential oils, lighting a candle, or creating a blend of aromatic herbs to help you relax and feel like you are at peace with yourself.

SOUND: You can play a relaxing playlist or any good music to help put you in a deeper meditative state.

TOUCH: You can hold crystals in the palm of your hand, or use a tool like a wand to direct energy for the sensation of touch. Grinding herbs in a mortar and pestle can also be a great way to get active with the sense of touch on your altar.

~ Chapter 6 ~

WITCHY WELLNESS:

YOUR BODY IS YOU

Witchcraft is rooted in wellness and healing. It can help you manifest the changes you want to make in yourself and the world around you. In Chapter 3 we jumped into how you can begin practicing self-love and beauty magic in the bathroom, and in Chapter 5 we looked at some of the ways you can use magic for the self; but these aren't the only ways to use witchcraft for wellness and acceptance. This section will dive further into magic for positivity, mindfulness, awareness, and being present with the help of natural ingredients. Once you understand these topics, you're another step closer to becoming your best witchy self.

Witchcraft and natural-healing practices often go together because they both help you become the best version of yourself. Wellness is the natural extension of these two practices and is a necessity for any modern witch, as practicing intentional lifestyle changes is essential for a healthy mind, body, and spirit.

Witchcraft also helps to empower the self and aids in discovering how to create change and transform your world. Through working with the self, you're one step closer to fulfillment and finding the answers to what you seek.

To be a perfect witch, you must first access your own inner power and be the conduit between your magic and the changes you seek. There's already a world of magic within your reach, and that begins with your mind–body connection.

Get ready to learn how to harness natural ingredients and spaces to practice witchy wellness, because your body is you.

SHOWER RINSES FOR POSITIVITY

Much like in Chapter 5, Magic with the Self, you can use magic for positivity and transformation. Spells cast in the shower are the easiest way to start working with your inner power while feeling soothed, uplifted, and energized. You can craft your shower rinse with any of the ingredients below. The miscellaneous ingredients below contain oats and honey for their soothing skin-care benefits and salt and sugar for their detoxifying benefits.

OPTIONAL POSITIVITY CORRESPONDENCES:

- **Herbs and botanicals:** Rose, lavender, mint, jasmine, thyme, lemon, chamomile

- **Crystals:** Turquoise, clear quartz, onyx, amethyst, jade, citrine, tiger's eye

- **Moon phases:** Full or waxing phases

- **Miscellaneous ingredients:** Oats, honey, sea salt, sugar

MAKING YOUR OWN RINSES:
1. Combine your ingredients into a jar and let soak for a few hours before your shower.
2. Strain into another jar or a bowl, and place near the shower.
3. During your shower, focus on your intentions for positivity and desired outcome, and pour the mixture over your body.

MIRROR AFFIRMATION WATERS FOR ACCEPTANCE

A mirror shouldn't be used only to look at your appearance. It's a powerful tool for casting spells to reflect your intentions. When you use a mirror to practice mindfulness and acceptance, you're raising energy to carry your intentions into your audience, which is you. This isn't any dif-

ferent from casting any other spell on a tool or vessel; it's just that the object or recipient has changed. You are now able to practice mindfulness in self-reflection and build your self-confidence. Use mirrors all around you to remind yourself of your own inner power, confidence, and talents.

MIRROR AFFIRMATION: On your mirrors at home, use floral, crystal, or moon-charged waters to create invisible sigils for different affirmations. Powering your waters will create stronger results. To get started, try "I accept myself unconditionally."

ACCEPTANCE CORRESPONDENCES:

- **Floral and herbal waters:** Lavender, chamomile, rosemary, garden sage

- **Crystal-infused waters:** Rose quartz, pink calcite

- **Moon charging:** Full or waning phases

MAKING YOUR OWN AFFIRMATION WATER:
1. Fill a jar with distilled or spring water.
2. Add a pinch of salt for cleansing, blocking negativity, and protection.
3. Then use your magic charging method of choice.

MOVEMENT AND BREATHWORK FOR MINDFULNESS

While we covered magic in a fitness setting and how to create pre-fitness rituals and set a safe and sacred space in Chapter 1, this chapter focuses on magic to explore the mind–body connection and how to alter your state of mind for your craft. When you focus on your mental and physical well-being, you open yourself up to a stronger and more intentional practice to cast spells from.

Ride a bike, lift weights, get on a treadmill, or practice yoga to craft a mindfulness practice that is uniquely yours. No matter which physical activity, focus your attention on your movement and breathwork that shifts your mental state from feeling distracted and busy to quiet, calm, and capable.

Mindfulness movement allows you to be present, release stagnant energy, and strengthen your mind–body connection. It's a great way to get yourself centered and uplifted before casting spells or practicing magic.

BREATHING: Observe your breath by purposely taking long, deep breaths to create calm, or short breaths for a short period to refresh.

STRETCHING OR YOGA: Release tension and repressed emotions through gentle stretching or movement, and allow yourself to be present.

HIGH INTENSITY: Nourish your muscles by turning up your workout to a high intensity through short bursts of cardio.

POTIONS FOR AWARENESS

From simple ingredients, you can easily create water- or syrup-based potions that are safe to consume. By combining potions and awareness practices, you can learn to be aware of deeper emotions.

Water-based potions are the easiest potions to make. They are herbal teas or powders dissolved in boiled water. Brew simple teas, or get creative and try making beverages like turmeric lattes, mushroom hot chocolate, or vanilla chai tea. Water-based potions have a shelf life of only up to twenty-four hours.

Syrup-based potions include creating an infusion of sugar or honey with water in an equal 1:1 ratio. You can also substitute the water for herb or botanical teas for different flavors. To use your honey potion, add it to a glass of water, or create cocktails and mocktail beverages. Syrup-based potions have a shelf life of three to six months.

AWARENESS REFLECTION: Begin making your potion by setting your intentions and gathering your ingredients. Then focus your attention on asking yourself the following questions while you enjoy your potion:

- What did you learn about yourself today?
- What impactful projects did you work on today?
- What new skill did you learn today?

GROUNDING IN THE PRESENT

Grounding is the act of reconnecting yourself to the earth, releasing excess stagnant energy, and being present in the moment. We often lead busy lives, and by consciously taking time away from your day-to-day and allowing yourself to reflect and analyze how your body feels, you can engage with the moment to create stronger and more intentional magic.

MEDITATION: Set time aside to close your eyes and visualize a warm, bright light at the top of your head. Practice deep breathing, and, with each inhale, visualize the light moving its way down through your body and into the ground.

SOIL: Collect a jar of dry soil to keep near or on your altar when you want to feel grounded. By touching soil from the earth, you strengthen your connection to it.

ESSENTIAL OILS: Mix patchouli, vanilla, cinnamon, bergamot, ylang-ylang, cedar, or fir essential oils in a carrier oil like olive, coconut, or jojoba, and apply a dot on your skin.

CRYSTALS: Use strong grounding herbs like hematite, red jasper, obsidian, or petrified wood. Hold the crystal in your hand and focus on harnessing its grounding energy and let it wash over your body.

EMOTIONS AND INTENTIONS

Spells are fueled by emotions and work with your focus, intention, and the power raised from the world around you. The more emotional energy you put into the spell, the more potent it will be.

Spells work best when you feel strongly about your desired outcome. If your heart isn't in it, your spell could fail. Intentions are the key that unlocks a spell's potential after you've raised your power or energy. They are the wishes or goals of your practice.

To manifest or attract your intended outcomes, take time in your witchcraft practice to set your intentions in your mind, out loud, or on paper. Without setting clear intentions, you're opening your practice to unclear and muddled wishes, which could rebound in unexpected ways like failed spells or by feeling strange energy surrounding you.

It's essential to be clear about what you want and why. Successful intention-setting can lead to the manifestation of your goals, positive changes in your life, and a connection to your intuition.

~ *Chapter I* ~

YOU AND YOUR
COVEN

n the simplest sense, covens are groups of witches who perform rituals, spells, and feasts. Covens aren't mandatory, but they can be helpful when you seek answers about your magic and practice.

Traditionally, covens were dedicated groups of witches who taught passed-down traditions and initiated new members. They sometimes had different levels or degrees of witch learning and member status, and were led by high priests and high priestesses. You might also see the terms pagan coven, Wiccan group, Druid grove, or heathen kindred. There are so many different types of groups that gather for different purposes.

The purpose of a coven is to bring witches together, create safe spaces to practice magic, promote unity, and foster learning. Some covens can also become like family.

Today, covens aren't as popular as they once were because of how many new paths a witch can take and how readily available information is.

You also don't need to follow any particular tradition to be a witch. Many witches prefer the solitary path for the freedom to practice however they want without any restriction.

The concept of a coven is still important today, but with social media and technology it's easier than ever to connect to other witches safely.

Through modernization, it's easier than ever to adapt the notion of a coven and create your own community—to host and attend witchy events and lunar circles. You can join a coven, or make your own. It's essential to make sure you can be yourself, share with like-minded individuals, and have fun.

⋙ SOLITARY WITCHCRAFT ⋘

Whether being part of a coven either isn't an option or of interest, there are still ways you can honor and announce your craft to yourself. The act of dedicating yourself to your practice is an important step in defining yourself as a witch, choosing your path, and setting your overall intentions. This is also a great way to begin personalizing your practice so it's uniquely yours.

SELF-DEDICATION RITUAL: During a new moon, which is the lunar phase for new beginnings, set aside about twenty minutes to perform a self-dedication ritual. This can be as simple as lighting a candle and meditating on what it means to be a witch, or as elaborate as crafting your own self-dedication oil, marking a sacred circle with salt or crystals, and creating a custom incantation. Whatever your practice centers around should be the focus.

BOOK OF SHADOWS: You can also begin a Book of Shadows, or, if you have one already, add a few pages about your practice. Writing about your practice is powerful and helps you define your craft and intentions.

LEAVING THE BROOM CLOSET

The "broom closet" refers to the symbolic place you hide your practice or beliefs from others. Many witches seek acceptance, validation, or emotional support from their loved ones, but witches are sometimes still perceived as evil because of their negative depictions in many religions. Choosing to not declare your practice doesn't make you less of a witch. You can be as secretive as you'd like. It's entirely your choice as to whether you want to tell others about your practice.

COMING OUT OF THE BROOM CLOSET: If you want to come out of the broom closet formally, first gauge the spiritual openness from those you want to tell. Are they generally open to or accepting of alternative practices? Another essential element to consider is your living situation. Are you underage? Live with parents or roommates? Don't jeopardize the roof over your head by announcing your beliefs; doing this may cause strain on your home life. Many witches wait to tell others until they are independent. Waiting until you are over eighteen is also often encouraged, to be taken more seriously as an adult. Adults can sometimes label your beliefs as a "phase" if you're still a teenager.

COMMUNITIES AND COVENS

With the use of hashtags and online groups on social-media channels, it's easier than ever to find other witches online. They also require hard work and dedication to thrive. Online settings often need a moderator or online host, basic technology experience, and responsiveness and hospitality from its members. If you're the host or moderator, it's important to keep your online community safe by establishing and enforcing community guidelines.

SEARCHING: Begin your search on social media platforms like TikTok, Instagram, and Twitter, searching terms and hashtags such as #witchesoftiktok, #witchesofinstagram, and #witchesoftwitter; and for other platforms like Facebook, Slack, and Discord, search for groups or channels with the name containing "witch."

SHARING: Be ready to share a little about your practice and what path you enjoy the most. If you encounter a toxic or unfriendly group, it's okay to walk away. You'll find one that's right for you. When you do find a group that's right for you, make sure to only partake in what you're comfortable with and to never share any personal information with others.

LUNAR CIRCLES AND WITCHY EVENTS

Lunar circles and witchy events are a great way to connect with fellow witches. You can often find in-person or online circles, events, and meetups. They allow you to find support and align with your beliefs.

ONLINE EVENTS: With the rise of video-conferencing apps, Reddit groups, WitchTok, and blogging, online events are more accessible than ever. Witches from all over the world can connect and create magic together. You can also look up the pagan sabbats, major celestial events, or the moon phases to begin your search for online events, circles, or meetups.

 # WORKSHOPS

Not sure if a coven is right for you, but still want to learn something new from other witches? Find a local or online workshop in an area of witchcraft. You can easily find witchy workshops for crafting spells or magical items. What's great about taking workshops is that you can take what works for you and leave the rest—because, remember, your practice is yours. If you feel drawn to a particular area of witchcraft, try searching for meetups or workshops. You'll be surprised at how many other witches probably have the same interests. Not sure where to start? Try any of the topics and types of witchcraft suggested below.

HOUSE WITCHCRAFT: Magic in or near the home. It includes kitchen, cottage, hearth, garden, and urban practices.

NATURE: This magic incorporates nature. It includes green and water magic, along with other focused practices like sea, weather, fire, air, crystal, fairy, and elemental.

TRADITIONAL OR PAGAN: Magic with older or more "traditional" roots. Practices incorporate folklore, deity, cultural aspects, and pagan practices. See also hedge, spirit work, shadow work, Old World, ceremonial, and Wicca.

ECLECTIC: Modern or niche magical practices that include working with astrology, divination, wellness, or symbols. These include cosmic, intuitive, tarot, glamour, wellness, secular, sigil, and lunar practices.

WHAT IS WICCA?

*W*icca is a modern pagan religion created by Gerald Gardner in the middle of the twentieth century that draws from ancient pagan traditions and focuses on ritual practices. Wicca is a duotheistic religion that honors both a god and a goddess. It certainly isn't unusual to see eclectic or broader practices of Wicca range from polytheism to goddess monotheism as well.

Wicca is sometimes practiced side-by-side with witchcraft practices to incorporate deity or faith. Wicca practices more rituals than spells and often involves rules surrounding will and karma. Wiccans follow a rede, or basic tenets that state "An' it harm none, do as ye will," which is a moral code. Witchcraft isn't Wicca and doesn't have to follow any rules or structures. Witchcraft can also be secular or accompanied by other religions or faiths.

~ Chapter 8 ~

MAGICAL

OBJECTS

Tools are a great way to amplify your magic for rituals or casting spells, but they aren't required.

Tools and objects are not inherently magical; they simply help you channel your energy and intent.

Many witches use different tools, depending on what they're drawn to. If you feel more drawn to green witchery, you'll probably have more herbs and spices, crystals, apothecary jars, and a mortar and pestle. If you feel more drawn to moon witchery, you'll probably have a moon-phase tracker, moon journals, and digital apps. These are two examples of how customized your practice could be.

Some of the most popular types of tools that you'll see other witches using are altarpieces, journals like Books of Shadows or grimoires, crystals and stones, herbs and flowers, candles, and incense.

You can find most witchcraft tools at in-person or online metaphysical shops, marketplace stores, or bulk-discount chains. You don't always have to buy tools. You can also create your own versions using household materials or items from craft stores.

Open your kitchen drawers and cupboards to see what you can use. You'll be surprised at what you can come up with. Always remember, your tools are uniquely yours, so get as creative, extravagant, or thrifty as you'd like with them.

⇛ ALTARS AND OBJECTS ⇚

An altar is a platform or table that serves as a workspace for spells and other magical practices. You can designate an area in any room of your home, create a travel altar for witchcraft on the go, or create altars outdoors.

The tools on your altar will differ depending on the traditions or pathways you follow. Pathways are the different types of witchcraft like green, water, elemental, cottage, kitchen, and many others. You can include any items you want. For suggestions, use any of the items recommended in the following pages.

Don't worry if creating an altar seems daunting or expensive. You can create an altar on any budget—as long as it's functional, it can be as simple or complex as you'd like.

BUDGET ALTAR IDEAS: Budget altars exist using matches for the element of fire, soil from the ground near your home or table salt for the element of earth, a wand from a fallen twig or incense for the element of air, and bowls of water for the element of water. You can make charm bags from old clothing fabrics and use a permanent marker to mark sigils on paper or stones.

ALTAR CUSTOMIZATION: Many witches choose to customize their altar to match a specific spell or complement a month or season. For example, if you want to cast a spell for love, you might wish to add rose petals or symbols of love to your altar. Preparing your altar should be fun, so feel free to let your creativity flourish.

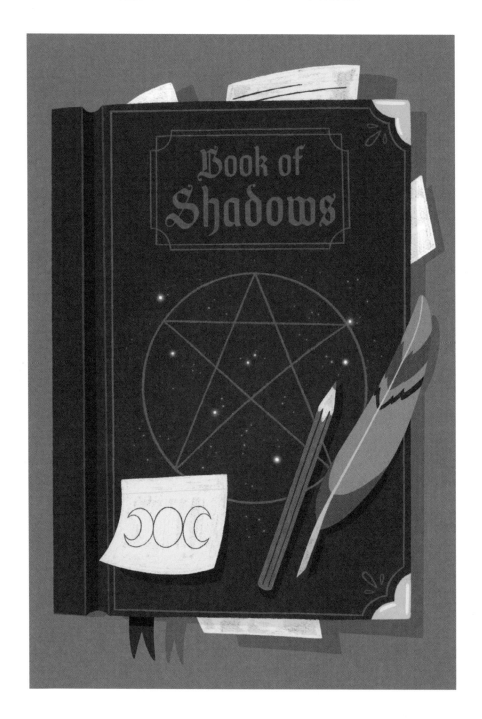

BOOKS OF SHADOWS AND GRIMOIRES

Many witches use journals to record their practice, writing down spells, rituals, meditations, recipes, readings, and notes. These journals are often called a Book of Shadows or a grimoire. These journals assist with the growth of your practice and provide a chance to discover and grow your knowledge.

Although a Book of Shadows and a grimoire are both journals, a Book of Shadows is often more personal than a grimoire, containing private notes about a witch's magic. Grimoires usually contain formal notes about spells and don't include anything personal. You can have one or the other, or both.

YOUR BOOK: This sacred tool houses the core elements of your path, and it can be as personalized as you'd like. Try making a Book of Shadows for trial-and-error spells and a grimoire for finalized spells and correspondences. Your Book of Shadows or grimoire can be hand-bound, in a binder, or even digital. The options are endless, and you can be as creative as you'd like. It's important to note that it's a book of your journey as a witch and should be taken care of and cherished. For suggestions on types of spells, visit Chapter 9. When creating your own Book of Shadows, remember to have fun!

⇛ CRYSTALS AND STONES ⇚

Crystals and stones are popular tools in witchcraft, as they have a wide range of uses. Crystals are used for healing, manifestation, and energy work. Stones are great to mark with symbols or sigils. While many spells recommend many different crystals and stones, you can start out with just a clear quartz crystal, since it can be used in place of other crystals in almost every spell.

Crystals can also be used for divination and crystal arrangements, or incorporated into witchcraft tools to amplify their energy. Some witches use crystals to physically mark or define boundaries for spell-casting a protection or sacred circles too.

Every crystal is unique, so a guidebook or list of crystal correspondences can be handy when choosing which stones you want. And when you use crystals, they often need to be cleared with water or smoke, and charged with energy from you or the moon between uses. The most powerful moon phase for charging is the full moon, so mark your calendar.

GENERAL CRYSTAL COLORS:

- **Yellow crystals** assist with the mind, communication, and logic.

- **Blue crystals** assist with emotions, intuition, and healing.

- **Green crystals** assist with wealth, success, and peace.

- **Red crystals** assist with vitality, energy, and passion.

HERBS, TREES, AND BOTANICALS

All kinds of plants are used for their flavorful or aromatic properties in food, medicine, fragrance, and magic. There are properties in every plant that can be harnessed to heal and guide you in your witchcraft. From the roots found underground to the leaves resting on the tallest trees, all plant life can be used in your practice.

When beginning to work with herbs, trees, and botanicals, start locally. What plants are native to your surrounding city? You can brew, mix, and grind a variety of leaves, barks, stems, and flowers for making magical preparations like teas, oils, and powders for incense, charms, and spells.

TEAS: A basic recipe for using culinary herbs or botanicals: mix one to two teaspoons with boiling water and let steep for five to ten minutes. The hardier the herb, the longer the steep time.

OILS: You can make basic herbal oils by placing your desired dried plant material in a jar and cover with oils like olive, almond, grapeseed, avocado, or apricot kernel and let sit for four to six weeks. For instant oils, you can use a few drops of essential oil instead of dried plants.

CHARMS: For most charms, grind dried herbs, barks, and botanicals, and mix them together into charm bags or jars.

≫ CANDLES AND INCENSE ≪

Candles can add power to spells and assist with energy work or divination. You can either dress candles with oils and decorate with herbs, or carve them with symbols and sigils.

Candles allow you to connect with energy around you, which is why candle magic is one of the easiest ways to jump into witchcraft. When burned with intention, candles take your desires and amplify your thoughts.

BURN TIMES AND CANDLE TYPES: Larger candles have a longer burn time. When you begin to work with candles, smaller ones like tealights, votives, or chimes are best. It's important to use an unburned candle for your new spells, so you don't mix old energies or intentions

with your current spell. As a general rule, 5- to 7-inch pillar candles will burn for 90 to 100 hours, smaller votive candles will burn for 10 to 15 hours, 12-inch taper candles will burn for 9 to 12 hours, and tealights will burn for just 4 to 6 hours.

Incense is another tool similar to candles that helps set the atmosphere, but incense can also banish negative energy. Incense is often used for cleansing, purifying, and setting intentions.

INCENSE VARIETIES: Incense can be either combustible or non-combustible. Combustible incense contains saltpeter to help it burn and comes in the form of store-bought cones, sticks, and coils. Non-combustible incense has to be burned on a charcoal disc. It usually comes in the form of loose incense mixes. Get creative with your magical objects and trust your intuition.

WHERE TO CAST A SPELL

The location of your spell can be just as important as your ingredients or magical tools. The location you choose can invite either peace and harmony, or chaos and the unexpected. Make sure to also practice your craft somewhere that makes you feel comfortable and safe.

You can dedicate an area of your home to create a sacred space and altar, or you can change it each time you craft a spell.

You might even want to cast some spells in different parts of your home. Perhaps a spell in the kitchen, one in the bathroom, a bedroom, or even outside your home. There's no wrong area to practice magic. What's important is your intention behind choosing the space. Is it for convenience? Quiet? Natural energy?

No matter where you choose to craft and cast your magic, be sure to always use your intuition and intention to guide you.

THE ROLE
OF THE MOON

NEW MOON: The new moon offers limitless potential and a clean slate. As such, this phase is perfect for spells relating to new beginnings, personal improvement, manifestation, peace, and divination.

WAXING MOON: A waxing moon means the moon is getting larger. This phase is perfect for spells that use growth energy, such as creativity, luck, courage, health, finances, balance, motivation, and love.

FULL MOON: The full moon occurs when the moon is round and at full brightness in the sky and is at its strongest. The full moon phase is perfect for spells relating to spirituality, charging, decisions, health, and success.

WANING MOON: A waning moon means the moon is decreasing in size. It's the perfect time to perform spells relating to grounding, release, eliminating, banishing, transitions, obstacles, and balance.

DARK MOON: Before the new moon, there's a dark or balsamic moon where the moon is not visible in the night sky. The dark moon phase is ideal for spells relating to intuition, banishing, protection, cleansing, meditation, and energy work.

~ Chapter 9 ~

SPELLS

S pells allow you to practice magic. They help create change in your life and bring out more confidence in yourself. Spells come in many different types:

- Attracting and invoking spells
- Stopping and halting spells
- Banishing and casting-out spells
- Absorbing and charging spells
- Charms and representation spells

If you begin here, you can start thinking of ideas for your spells. Do you want more wealth? Then perhaps try an attracting spell. If you want to stop a streak of bad luck, then try a halting spell.

Once you learn to identify the different types of spells that you want to cast, you can start looking at correspondences for your ingredients. If you frequently cast money spells, you might want to keep on hand mint, basil, green crystals, bay leaves, or other symbols of money like coins.

ATTRACTING AND INVOKING SPELLS

Many of the attracting or invoking spells involve love, prosperity, and positivity. They are spells that draw to you or manifest change. To enhance the power of any of your attracting and invoking spells, you can incorporate more correspondences or spell-timing, like moon phases.

ATTRACTING-CHARM SPELL: You can craft a charm with ingredients charged with your intentions. You can use drawstring bags, small bottles, or boxes to house your charm ingredients. For love, use flower petals like rose, pink or red crystals, and spices like cinnamon or ginger.

INVOKING-CHANT SPELL: An invoking spell is a great way to use fewer ingredients but still cast powerful magic. For a basic invoking spell, create a chant, prayer, or incantation with meaning. Use words like "I draw to me" or "I call forth." You don't have to make your words rhyme, unless you enjoy it. Rhyming can sometimes be fairly advanced. Many witches cast invoking spells to call on the elements, create a sacred circle, or voice their intentions aloud.

STOPPING AND HALTING SPELLS

Stopping and halting spells are used to stop gossip, stealing, and habits you want to break. These spells don't cause harm to others, but instead stop the offense or negativity in its tracks. You can also use these types of spells for better sleep by stopping nightmares or halting unwanted noises. Many of these spells utilize herbs, spices, candle magic, incantations, words or sigils, and the element of ice.

NIGHTMARES: Halt nightmares and prevent them from recurring by crafting a dream sachet or charm bag filled with herbs. Try a mixture of lavender, chamomile, thyme, and bay laurel.

GOSSIP: Craft a spell jar with gossip-halting spices like clove and black pepper, and carry it with you to end gossip. Loosely grind them to activate and release their aromas before adding them to your jar. You can also add salt to amplify the jar's power and, if you have space in your spell jar, add a small piece of paper with your intention. You can also write your intentions to stop gossip and place the paper in your freezer. Try to be as detailed as you can about the gossip to enhance the effectiveness.

BANISHING AND CASTING-OUT SPELLS

Banishing spells differ from stopping spells because they don't just halt things, they send them away from you. Banishing and casting-out spells are ideal for sending away negative or unwanted energy. Many banishing spells incorporate the elements. Use incense for air, candles for fire, consecrated water for water, and soil for earth. You could combine all the elements, or use them individually to craft your own banishing spell.

FIRE SPELL: On a piece of paper, write down what you want to banish, and light a candle. Light the edge of the paper on fire inside a fire-safe bowl like a cast-iron cauldron, and let the paper burn out in the bowl.

AIR SPELL: Use a banishing incense made with ingredients like pepper, clove, dragon's blood, thyme, basil, cedar, or rosemary. Light the incense and write or say your intentions, and let the incense carry your intentions into the air.

WATER SPELL: In a bowl of water, add one teaspoon of salt and stir until combined. Focus on your intentions as you stir. Take the bowl of water outdoors to use, but try not to pour the mixture on plants, as salt could harm them. Create a chant or incantation to say as you sprinkle the water around your feet.

EARTH SPELL: Focus on your intentions and write what you want to banish on a piece of paper or a bay leaf. Bury the note in the ground under a layer of soil.

ABSORBING AND CHARGING SPELLS

Absorbing and charging spells are great for increasing your energy. You can either absorb energy directly or use charging spells on crystals or water. Creating a charged crystal or water is a great way to store energy for later use. These spells are great for attracting or invoking spells, because you can customize what types of properties you want in the energy.

CENTERING: Centering is a great way to get into raising or absorbing energy for spells. It's strongest when used in conjunction with meditation and even breathing techniques. Sit in a comfortable place and position, and focus on your connection to the ground. Visualize a thread of energy connecting you to the earth below your feet, whether directly or 50 feet through an apartment floor. Once the connection is made, see that thread of energy fill your being.

CHARGING: Place a crystal or jar of water overnight on a windowsill that would get exposed to the full moon. You could also place items outside in a yard if you feel it would be safe. This will charge with energy of the most powerful moon phase to use in any spell.

CHARM AND REPRESENTATION SPELLS

Charm and representation spells allow you to connect symbolism to objects or people. These spells are often associated with sympathetic magic, or magic connected through imitation or correspondences. Poppets are popular forms of sympathetic magic to connect spells to people.

Charm spells don't need to be as specific as poppets, and can be used to create jars or charm bags with layers of ingredients like crystals, herbs, spices, salts, and symbols. You can write down words or symbols too, to add to the charm. The more ingredients you have, the more correspondences or meanings you can attach to a charm. For example, if you want a charm for love, you could fill a jar with rose petals; but if you want a charm for self-love, you can use pink rose petals, a rose quartz crystal, and some healing salts like Himalayan for a more potent, focused charm.

POPPET SPELL: To use a poppet to help you heal from sickness, sew a doll with needle and thread. Fill the doll with cotton, herbs, and symbols of yourself. You could use a string of hair, a small photo of yourself, and healing herbs like ginger, nettle, valerian root, or chamomile.

SPELL TIMING

*W*itches often plan spells for the different days of the week, to connect with the energy of the planets. By doing so, you might find that your spells will become more powerful during a specific day.

- **MONDAY**
  Planet: The Moon
  Energy: Dreams, family, intuition, wisdom, messages, illusion, divination, water magic, cleansing, renewal, sleep, peace, emotions

- **TUESDAY**
  Planet: Mars
  Energy: Success, conflict, initiation, strength, victory, courage, defense, wards, protection, competition, ambition, psychic attacks, skill

- **WEDNESDAY**
  Planet: Mercury
  Energy: Communication, creativity, messages, luck, travel, perception, learning, trade, business, money, divination

- **THURSDAY**
  <u>Planet:</u> Jupiter
  <u>Energy:</u> Abundance, power, luck, fortune, health, prosperity, contracts, business, authority, blessings, legal matters, fertility, desires, home

- **FRIDAY**
  <u>Planet:</u> Venus
  <u>Energy:</u> Love, romance, marriage, fertility, sexual matters, healing, protection, beauty, friendship, growth, attraction, sympathy, reconciliation, self-love, mirrors, crafts

- **SATURDAY**
  <u>Planet:</u> Saturn
  <u>Energy:</u> Meditation, psychic skills, defense, freedom, communication, spirits, protection, wisdom, cleansing, negativity, patience, grief

- **SUNDAY**
  <u>Planet:</u> The Sun
  <u>Energy:</u> Success, creativity, hope, self-expression, fortune, fame, wealth, exorcism, leadership, joy, renewal, change, health, vitality, growth, clarity, affirmations

SPELL SUBSTITUTIONS

One of the most intimidating aspects of casting spells is the ingredients. What if you can't find wolfsbane, jasmine, or saffron? You can easily find substitutions for your spells based on purpose, aroma, or intuition. Sometimes trusting yourself is the best way to make a substitution for your spell.

For example, if you need nutmeg for a money spell but you don't have it, it's time for some substitutions. Take some notes on the color, smell, and size of the herbs and spices you need to substitute. Nutmeg, when ground, looks like powdered cinnamon. Both have similar strong aromatics, are warming, and are similar colors. Powdered ginger could also be a good substitution for these same reasons. Although lighter in color, it has aromatic and warming properties.

If you also needed mint for that money spell and do not have any, take notes about its qualities. It's green and soft, and has a light distinctive aroma. Great substitutions include basil, lemon balm, rosemary, and sage. Another important note about these herbs is that they all belong to the mint family.

~ *Chapter 10* ~

CHOOSE YOUR
ANIMAL

The association of witches and animals means they have long been intertwined throughout history—in folklore, shamanic practices, and traditions from all around the world. This connection can be summarized as: an animal with whom a witch has a special bond, but there's more to this than many realize.

Between the fifteenth and seventeenth centuries, witches in Europe were said to have entities or spirits that would assist them in their craft. These beings were often said to be in the form of an animal—such as the more popularly known black cat. The notorious cat, depending on which point we look at in history, is seen as either lucky or unlucky.

In ancient Egypt, cats were considered lucky and patrons of the goddess Bastet, symbolizing immortality and longevity. The change from lucky to unlucky happened when Christianity began to spread in Europe and Egypt. It became illegal to practice any form of pagan religion, and the black cat was identified as a part of pagan beliefs. A decree was issued by the Roman emperor Theodosius that the worship of household-guardian spirits was strictly forbidden. Those caught with black cats were persecuted. Fast-forward to today: cats are often seen as animal companions for witches, due to the events in history.

Animal allies can actually be any animal, not just a cat. They might be your pet or a spirit visiting you, either in physical form or in the dream or astral realms. Any animal that you choose to work with and that chooses to work with you can help provide clarity, inspiration, and protection to your spells. This relationship is built on trust and friendship. These connections can create a lasting impact on your practice in positive ways.

FAMILIARS

The word *familiar* comes from the Latin *familiaris,* which means "servant," or that which "belongs to a family or household." While familiars were historically known as witches' servants, today they are known as the witch's companion. The companionship built between a familiar and a witch should be mutually beneficial and respected.

Having a familiar shouldn't feel one-sided but rather a relationship of mutual exchange in services like assistance with spell work or goods like food or shelter. The familiar, in return, is more inclined to assist with magical tasks.

YOUR FAMILIAR: To confirm whether you already have a familiar, or to know what to look for in a familiar, pay attention to the following:

- You feel an immediate connection with an animal.
- An animal or pet has randomly visited you and returned.
- You understand an animal or pet, and it understands you.
- If you live with others, the animal or pet has a bond only with you.
- Your intuition tells you it's a familiar.

 # FETCHES

Fairly similar in concept was the fetch, which often refers to an apparition of a person, spirit double, or wraith. A wraith is said to be a spirit or ghostlike image of someone. The use of *fetch* is prevalent in European practices, and is a way of manifesting one's desire. It comes from the central idea that you can separate a part of yourself for certain purposes.

The fetch is an assistant to a practitioner, much like the familiar. It's an entity that fulfills the wishes of a witch.

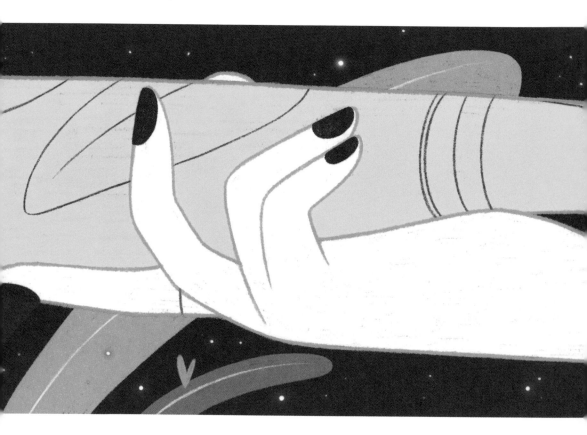

Fetches can also be used to project a witch's double into astral flight or out-of-body experiences. This is often used in hedge-riding practices. The fetch can assist a witch in astral flight: guiding, protecting, and assisting a practitioner.

ASTRAL REALM: To begin working with fetches in the astral realm, you need to first be comfortable with a meditation practice. Once you are comfortable with that practice, the next step is to introduce trancelike states through self-hypnosis. After that, you can begin visualizing your astral form or fetch. Try reading other texts on astral projection before attempting to take flight for astral safety.

SPIRIT ANIMALS AND ANIMAL GUIDES

While the concept of a spirit animal, totem, or animal guide has been around for a while, the term *spirit animal* didn't come about until the 1980s, when pagan and Wiccan practices began using the term. And it wasn't until the 1990s that the term began to be used in pop culture. Many indigenous North American cultures use totems, which refers to an animal kinship or symbol of a family or clan. If we look to Indigenous cultures in historical Mesoamerica, we'll find the mention of a nagual, which refers to a personal guardian spirit, ally, or helper spirit. The specific uses of totems and naguals are sacred to these Indigenous cultures and are considered closed practices, meaning they were created for that culture specifically. Be careful never to take from closed practices.

What all these spirits or entities have in common is the specific relationship between a person and a spirit, regardless of its form. Today we often see relationships with animal types and spirits. This is thanks to the symbolism and meaning found in every animal species.

SPIRIT ORACLES: If you have an interest in the symbolism of spirits and animals, seek out a spirit oracle divination deck. These decks are created to assist you with working with the symbolic representation of animal guides in your practice.

FAIRIES AND FATES

Fairies (or "faeries") take on countless forms, and many tales of fairies can be traced back throughout time. The term *fairy* comes from Latin *fata*, meaning "the Fates," which is the plural of *fatum*, meaning "destiny" or "fate." In Greek, Roman, and Norse mythologies, fairies were related to the goddesses of fate. Parallels between cultures around the world can be seen when it comes to the weavers of fate. Fairies were often associated with springs, wells, and quiet, natural places, which were often given offerings and sought out for their blessings in fate.

Throughout the blurring of history, fairies were also connected to the goddesses of birth, life, death, fertility, and protection. They are often symbolized with spinning wheels, spiderwebs, and other forms of thread.

FAIRY WALK: Take a walk on a trail or anywhere where trees are abundant, and sit quietly. Allow the feeling of the sentience of life to wash over you. Connect with the energy. As an option, craft a natural offering to bring with you for blessings associated with your fate. You can use raw honey, bake honey cakes, pour a cup of milk, sprinkle white almonds, or even craft a floral arrangement.

⋙ ELEMENTAL BEINGS ⋘

The four classical elements of earth, air, water, and fire are very prominent in witchcraft practices. They are connected to cardinal directions, seasons, timing, zodiac signs, and other correspondences. These elements have also been interwoven in folklore, mythology, and literature, presenting themselves in beings and spirits reminding witches of the importance of nature. An elemental familiar can present itself to you through nature, in spirit, or in objects and symbols. You can use elemental beings to connect with the energy of the natural world through any of the ways listed next.

EARTH

Direction: North

Elemental: Gnomes

Zodiac Signs: Capricorn, Virgo, Taurus

Season: Winter

Time of Day: Midnight

Stage of Life: Old Age

WATER

Direction: West

Elemental: Undine

Zodiac Signs: Cancer, Pisces, Scorpio

Season: Fall

Time of Day: Sunset

Stage of Life: Maturity

AIR

Direction: East

Elemental: Sylphs

Zodiac Signs: Gemini, Libra, Aquarius

Season: Spring

Time of Day: Dawn

Stage of Life: Birth

FIRE

Direction: South

Elemental: Salamanders

Zodiac Signs: Aries, Leo, Sagittarius

Season: Summer

Time of Day: Noon

Stage of Life: Youth

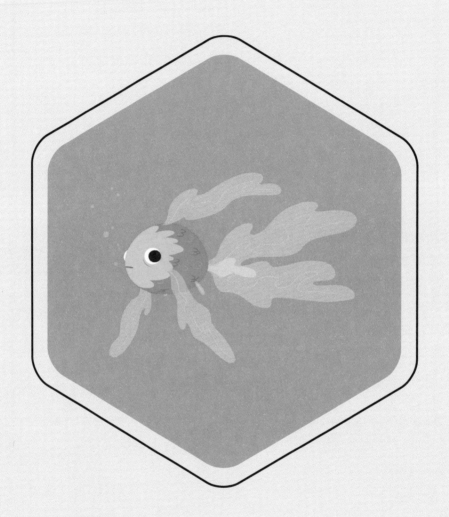

PET FAMILIARS

*P*ets are domesticated animals like dogs and cats that could become your familiar or witchcraft companion; but there are also less-common pets such as fish, birds, rodents, or reptiles.

- **DOGS:** Dogs symbolize unconditional love and loyalty, safeguarding, devotion, fidelity, and faith. They're also reliable protectors and a symbol of truthfulness to yourself.
- **CATS:** Cats symbolize various aspects such as intuition, curiosity, protection, elegance, independence, freedom, enlightenment, balance, and hope. They are also wise and a symbol of witchcraft.
- **FISH:** Fish create a strong connection to the water element and are symbols of the depths of the unconscious, purification, healing, and emotions. They are also related to knowledge, transformation, creativity, and femininity.
- **RODENTS:** Because of their size, rodents symbolize the possibilities in life and the ability to accomplish or adapt to anything, regardless of their circumstances. They also have a strong connection to the earth.
- **REPTILES:** Many reptiles shed their skins and symbolize regeneration, immortality, and the cycle of life. Like rodents, they are also often linked to the element of earth and sometimes fire.

NOTES

NOTES

NOTES

NOTES

AMBROSIA HAWTHORN is a witch, founder of *Witch-ology Magazine*, author of *The Spell Book for New Witches*, *Seasons of Wicca*, and *The Wiccan Book of Shadows*. She is also a tarot reader, astrologer, and herbalist. Ambrosia's practice is eclectic, and she focuses her craft on the connection between the natural world and inner power. Ambrosia also hosts witchcraft classes at Venefica Cottage.

GIULIA VARETTO is an Italian illustrator based in Milan. The primary sources of inspiration for her works are nature and magic. She explores the connection between humans and the natural world through fairy-tale and dreamlike illustrations. Her curiosity and passion for witchcraft and esotericism led her to discover the folklore and mythology of the Wicca religion.